the myth of me

the myth of me

poems by

Centa Therese

© 2025 Centa Therese. All rights reserved.
This material may not be reproduced in any form, published,
reprinted, recorded, performed, broadcast,
rewritten, or redistributed without
the explicit permission of Centa Therese.
All such actions are strictly prohibited by law.

Cover design by Shay Culligan
Cover photo by Centa Therese
Author photo by Snappr

ISBN: 978-1-63980-728-4
Library of Congress Control Number: 2025935364

Kelsay Books
502 South 1040 East, A-119
American Fork, Utah 84003
Kelsaybooks.com

for my adult children, Corey and Arianna,
my inspiration to do *something*

Acknowledgments

Gratitude to the following journals, where earlier versions of these poems first appeared:

DrumVoices Revue: "Borderland"
Eclipse: "To My Daemon"
Tiny Lights: "Howarth Park; Between Rains"

Contents

I. Intersections

Return	15
Plethora of Bloom	16
Mendocino Coast	17
Constellation	18
Doran Beach	19
After Light	20
Strange Familiars	21
Salt Spring	22
Anything Wingless	24
The Metaphysics of Facsimile	25
Windowless	26
Slant Lines of Rain	27
Off the Deer Path	28
Santa Rosa Creek	29
Intersection	30
Dream Repair	32
Upright in Questionable Air	33

II. Dark Charm

For All the Darkness	37
When There's Been No Praise	38
Dark Charm	39
Howarth Park Between Rains	40
Dark Charm II: Not an Apparition	41
Monkey Flower Ode	42
Larger Than in Life	43
Cul-de-sac	44
Along the Pond	45
Camp Solo	46
Old School	47
Early Light	48
Witness	49

III. Portals

Ode to Dream	53
Found Object	54
Release of the Missing Piece	55
Wooden Stars	56
Hamilton Cove	57
Portal of Inevitability	58
For Silence	59
All the World	60
Borderland	61
I Dream of the Last Resort	62
How to Argue with Time	63
Between Rooms	64
To My Daemon	65
The Potter	66
Crossroads	68
The Myth of Me	69
Wire Bird	70
Truth Is Darkest	71
You Are Not Lost	72
Around the Corner	73
Aperture	74
Paean	75
Make My Day	76
Up the Inside Passage	78
Welcome This Artifact	79
Another COVID Day	80
Enshrined	82
Bardo	83
Reverse Gravity	85

In sleep, my four-year-old daughter says,
Everything is lost. Fallen. Dead. This is gone.

Dharma: that which supports, upholds; that which
Remedies, alleviates, heals, and restores.
—Lama Surya Das

I. Intersections

Return

The walnut tree is not separate from
the light that greens its leaves,
nor from the crow perched on a wire
over four-way traffic, a full walnut in its beak,
nor from the nut bursting, the silent
explosion of shell scattering in its slow,
buoyant descent.

Canada Geese come in autumn to graze
by the lake, and when they disappear
you think they're gone forever—
yet they return for days before taking final leave
of the drying foothills, their liquid
intelligence reshaping the air.

Plethora of Bloom

Drawn to magenta, your body stops
by a plethora of its bloom.

You note the ache back-of-the-knees,
when swept away by high rustling.

Once, you heard only duck talk,
dry leaves scattering, singing air.

And, dipping the tip of your brush in
deep-to-delicate grays, then painting a face,

it was a new face that emerged.
When lights flickered in hills beyond

the narrow streets you walked along,
you thought *I'm not the same as I ever was!*

Then, right before you opened your eyes,
you were half convinced

the place you yearned to be, you'd
never been until now.

Mendocino Coast

Spring at the headlands: ambling through
fields of yellow broccoli, dusty-purple cabbage,

pale radish stalk to the cliff's edge,
where below, redwood stumps drifted in

and out with the tide. The climb down to
the rocky shore: the parched grin of a

whalebone, seals at the mouth of the Navarro.
The single glass on the windowsill, and you,

reminding me how we are meant to
be in surprise, like the sheet rolled back

to reveal two missing blue socks—
we aren't to know a thing before it arrives,

so the foothold enters us unnamed,
ourselves being the clay this world hollows out.

Constellation

Born in gray light, silhouettes of fir
pierce the dawn sky. No one can say who
the mother is, but color comes.

One bird trills into the silence. As with dying,
no one can say precisely why or when,
but death comes.

Most mornings, I drink coffee from a cup
I made, sitting at the window in a blue
velveteen chair and listening to the birds.

Every weekend I leave my children, or they
leave me. I want to say *Don't you worry. No one
is exempt from this heartache.*

Born in gray light, some children migrate
between seasons, or households, through war
of one sort or another, waiting for the sun to

fully rise, waiting for us to realize what is
ours to carry. No one can tell us.
We can't tell them. None of it we call home.

Doran Beach

Along the fog-enclosed bay, surfers in black
rubber suits haul finned boards into the waves.

In the uprooted drift, crescent shards of clam shell,
hollowed orange crab backs, dismembered claws,

slick green ribbonings of seagrass, an old rubber
sole, and the carcass of a wild boar—

the blunt snout protruding from the skull, sharp
incisors, and sunken eyeholes in a mask of dry,

shrunken hide. Flanks of twisted driftwood, clusters
of brown soap bubbles nestled in tangled tubes of

seaweed, strips of torn black plastic. Emerged from
the fog, houses barnacle gray-green hills, and

in the dunes, tufts of grass sway—and at my feet,
impressed in the moist sand

an angel flanked by the twin arcs of
her wind-inscribed wings.

After Light

They sat in canvas chairs, facing
the horizonless night sea sky. Bone shaken,
she realized they'd been the unwitting

directors of a narrative fatefully cast, and
simultaneously the characters, absent
in the play of their lives.

Along the length of shoreline, beacon
outcroppings of whinstone bore witness
to the immensity of all they had failed,
in their singular lives, to see.

Next day, driving back along the river,
her passenger eye caught the fractured
afternoon light, as it tipped its brilliant
hat, flaring off a common street sign
into the bright-lettered sky.

Strange Familiars

First, Rat appeared, an aspect of herself
she had long despised, who needed her love.
Once embraced, he transformed, becoming
beautiful—self-loathing lost its foothold.

Night came when moonlight banked against
a rim of woods as Stag emerged. His body
staggering, young antlers swaying, too heavy
for his juvenile frame.

He zagged toward her car, drunk with rage,
wanting in. Instead of fleeing, she rolled down
the window and took his human hand in hers.

Bowed now toward the dark, Owl emerged.
The aspect of herself so long buried she might
as well have been a stranger, yet so vital that
without her, she was withered from her absence.

Ecstatic with longing for her birthright, she
reclaimed what was hers. Though rarely
addressed by name, she called her heart.

Salt Spring

I flew all the way to Vancouver to save
that friendship. In the guest room, I raised
the warped and splintered window in its
hundred-year-old frame:

In high school, we adopted rhyming nicknames,
twin mannerisms, contagious symbiotic giggles.

Winters, we both wore tweed midi-skirts and fur
coats—D, her mother's full-length ermine, and I,
a black rabbit jacket from the flea market. Our
outfits were complete in round-toed, knee-high
leather boots, shoulder bags, and long neck scarves
we crocheted ourselves.

When summer came, Joe the Sandal-maker
designed our sandals. (I always envied her
small feet and hands.) We styled our hair in tiny,
braided curls, looking enough alike to confuse
teachers, who took us to be sisters. For two only
children of divorced parents, it fit, exactly.

Our melded identities crafted a double fortress—
a mutual defense against forces that held us down, a
buffer against a freedom coming on too fast
and not fast enough, and from the vast, unwritten
future about to engulf our separate lives.

We ferried to Salt Spring on a mission to
break the silence, share old hurts, hopefully
to heal. While away, back on the mainland, a
sparrow flew in through the guest room window.
The one left open for the soul to fly free.

Anything Wingless

Anything can harm you. A sliver from a telephone
pole, a barbed wire fence, the wind if it pierces your
face, the sun if you look at it straight, or a door that
hacks through your finger bone.

It could be water that does it, buoyancy forgotten,
or a stick in the eye. Even the color blue from a
cornflower could rub your eyes blind if you let it:
Things outside your skin can be used against you.
A word. A look. A gesture.

I lie under the sheets stiff as the dead in their
coffins, so the spiders will be fooled and forget to
climb up my cold legs. I still my breathing until it
disappears—a wave hardening to stone in my chest.

I silence my sex before it knows its name, give it
another face, as if it were a face—as something
wingless knows only by dream what it is to fly.

The Metaphysics of Facsimile

In the light of a caramel flame, yoked in
luminous goo, she hunkers over metaphysics—
the facsimile of the egg she inhabits.

Gripping blue oars, a window appears.
Pressing her cheek to the fray, she notes
the passing scenery: flashing neon,
blazon billboards, fallen pinwheels,
and an old woman wearing red lipstick and
a flip style wig, knee-high black patent
leather boots with matching coat, walking
the sidewalk while scolding an irreverent
cat and yanking on his leash.

An iridescent bird morphs into a flock, then flies
off. A voice says, *Paint that, why don't you!*

Windowless

She eats her lunch in a field; in the heat
of October bees.

Excluded from the crowd she didn't ask
to be a part of, she wants a dramatic exit.

Waking daily with a dull pang of guilt,
doubt born of false consignment.

It's not a new story—the dog's incessant
barking at the dark, outside the empty house.

In class, a woman presents a painting she
claims to be the first of her own ideas.

Who would not yearn to enter the world
as if invited—to leave the window behind?

Slant Lines of Rain

Black-eyed Susans adorn rows of harvested corn—
thin straw skins folded in hollow prayer, behind
them, their newer growth.

From behind the wheel, I explain the scenery to my
four-year-old daughter—how the sideways drift of
the Nimbus—*See those gray stripes in the distance,
that's rain!* falling on the flat, green fields beyond.

Clearly, A does not see what I think I know, nor
does she fathom rain as separate from her, as we
are heading straight into it—now, pummeled under
the hoop of its wide skirt, engulfed in a sudden flash
of brightening sky, thunder at our tail.

Off the Deer Path

We thank pine, cedar, and juniper for their woody
cones, life-giving seeds, and shade; the earth for

supporting our bodies; our bodies for lending us
form to inhabit, without which the earth would not

be our inheritance. We thank the warm wind's rustle
through branches; aromatic sagebrush—

home to bobcat, coyote, elk, and innumerable
species of birds. We are grateful for our

meandering footsteps on and off the deer path,
for our drumbeat, and the nest we find—

a fallen cup, spiraling galaxy of grass woven
into grass—where we stop to rest in a congregation

of tall stupas and bask in sunlight; and where,
hanging from the tip of a pine limb, sap sparkles

on a long hanging cone, under which we sing,
high and low in a language fresh and unknown.

Santa Rosa Creek

After days of heavy winter rain, the sky is clear,
the water, quiet. Beneath the overpass, a shopping
cart lies on its side in trampled grass. Inhabited by
mallards and egrets, the algae filled creek gurgles
at a rocky pass.

Wind-blown grasses wrap dying stalks, bent like old
women bowed to winter. Finches populate the trees,
dart from oak to bay and back again. Flotsam, like
flypaper, clings to spines of dying fennel.

Along the concrete embankment, strips of black
plastic thread the bush, lean in towards the water.
Wind and rain-beaten bags lie on the ground like
old skins, tattered drapery, dropped wings.

A few leaves cling to stripped branches, taper
toward the sun. Grit, starched filament,
tumbleweed, bouquets of pungent new growth.
Brown pods hang precariously—three-sided
purses spilled of seed, and rippling grasses
sketch the water's surface like a lover's scribe.

Intersection

Where Farmer's Lane dead-ends at the Flamingo
Hotel, two black butterflies flutter toward one
another, loop, cross in figure eights then veer
off in separate directions.

A young man pushes a blue racing bike,
stepping off the curb. An old man follows,
in a yellow shirt and blue baseball cap—his face
bent long-jawed into his shaggy white beard, he
lumbers his way from one side of the crosswalk to
the other.

Stopped at the light, in a dusty gray car, a third man
adjusts his mirror and begins to shave with battery-
operated razor—tinny violins blasting from the car
radio—as he waits for the light to turn.

Clambering up from a homeless encampment under
the proximal bridge, another man followed by a
rooster, passes under a tree boasting of yellow
blossoms—both arrived together at the crosswalk.

In the center divide, stands yet a fifth man holding
up a poster-board sign saying HUNGRY and NEED
WORK, greeting each stalled car as he panhandles
holding out his hat, asking God for Mercy, and
bowing to anyone who offers a few pennies.

Where Farmer's Lane and the Flamingo Hotel intersect, and the highway veers right and continues.

Dream Repair

My mother stands near, a quiet, wispy presence
she never was, dropped in from the afterlife,
having misplaced her linchpin of rage.

My father rolls up in a shiny black sedan, delivered
by chauffeur, and though he needs help getting out
of the car, his thick curls have gone back, for the
day, to black.

Ringing in from the airport, my stepmother
kvetches about having to wait. I assure her she's
not been forgotten and will be picked up shortly.

My best friend from high school's mother, steps
out of a limo wearing pumps and a floozy dress,
looking a good deal younger than when last we saw
her, at the hospital, as she was being wheeled
passed us on a gurney, exclaiming, *There's no exit!*

Whoever divined this reunion knew well to invite
her daughter, who's had a change of heart
apparently, as she is arriving on the next flight,
to be with everyone by dinnertime.

I wake to find myself sobbing, feeling the chasm
between reconciliation and too many days spent
kicking small stones along a rim of ground,
as it erodes underfoot.

Upright in Questionable Air

After newspapers announced that ice had
been discovered on the moon, he announced
that he would live to see space stations on
the moon, interplanetary travel, artificial wood or
water reinvented from Jupiter's elements,
and humans occupying space millions of years
from now. He went on to say that he knew in his
bones the human drama has repeated through
countless eons and would continue to do so—
and because he was so certain, whatever she
thought she knew of existence—like moon ice—
cracked. She was only beginning to sense the
depth of her ignorance—
      to shiver upright in questionable air.

II. Dark Charm

For All the Darkness

Fear deceives, likes to dress up as some big
concern. Things are shaky, make no mistake.

A spine remains vertical for only so long.
People and situations are mostly a rub in which
everyone glamorizes their reason for being.

Why complicate? It's the season for waking
in the dark. Maybe you sleep alone, whether or
not a friend shares your bed.

Maybe life feels as chaotic as if it never was
possessed of order. You've lived a crapshoot; what's
left to fear?

Death is just an end game, orderly in its way.
Where you struggle, it completes things.
Decisive, it won't change its mind on you.

Whatever vows you've broken, whatever
island of distrust you find yourself shipwrecked on,
thank the lonely night for all the darkness

you rest in, in which to realize your life.

When There's Been No Praise

In a land where newspapers sell for bread,
and hands hang by a thread to the arms they
belong to, as the instinct for belonging has
faded from the pages of people's minds,
scarcity reigns.

This morning, Lack of Wonder appeared:
odd infants from dream, reminding me they
are mine to feed. Too soon on their feet, too
young for teeth; they leap over the bedposts
like acrobats, chase featherless birds,
malnourished cats.

When I don't heed their call, they flash their
monster eyes, gnash their terrible teeth. I wake
late in their bed, the sun near scorching the sky,
its constant light bleeding along the untended yard.

Dark Charm

That no one had told her he'd left for good—
at the betrayal . . . *the petals of its eyes never closed.*

She lifted the still limp body from the gutter,
draped it over rigid forearms, and stepped off
the curb into a story, into an untruth,

imagining herself one who'd answered the call—
a doctor, a rescuer come too late, or simply,
goodness itself. Like carrying the cloth over an
altar, she crossed the street and mounted the steep,
wood steps to the door.

In this way she delivered her dark charm.

Howarth Park Between Rains

Thick fistfuls of cloud press against keyholes
of blue; unexpected summer rain: Crow bats its
wings, swoops down towards the water, arcs
upward, descends onto a branch.

Grey sky illuminates the ducks' orange webbed feet.
Unlikely candidates for grace, their plump,
oval bodies waddle along the shore, green heads
twirling on supple necks, broad yellow bills
preening underwing.

In this park, we celebrated the children's first
birthdays. No pony rides today, merry-go-round
down, kids grown with families of their own.

Whitman once wrote: *The pleasures of heaven and
the pains of hell are with me. The first, I graft and
increase upon myself; the latter, I translate into a
new tongue.*

Between rains, moist air cloaks the skin with insular
affection. A mild breeze sweeps the lake's surface.
Ducks perch on rocks, nibble breadcrumbs by the
water.

Neither literary nor solitary; they aren't seeking the
missing key underwing or hidden in keyholes of
brightening sky. Hardy and tenacious, they primp
their feathers one by one,
        as if washing their own children.

Dark Charm II: Not an Apparition

A lamp-lit road, arched with old-growth Sycamore. In the middle of the street, poised inside a halo of lamplight, regal in his vertical posture, as if rising from a stone, throne, or emerged, a god, from the watery black depths.

The eyes flashed starlight; though, upon closer inspection, it was revealed to be the reflection from the hi-beams of the driver's car, now at full stop.

No, this was not a god. This was a creature who'd been run over; whose torso was hinged to flattened flanks, who'd been stopped by impact in mid-flight, still displaying terror in the eyes, neither dead nor alive, and risen, a dark charm, from a pool of his own black blood.

For the driver, the floodgates had flown open, unlocking vaulted memory. Her body, recently cut open to birth her firstborn, now experienced a second kind of surgery, a second kind of opening.

This death was also about the life she took when too young to claim her power, and the agony she births now, is for every shocked, helpless, terminally wounded, eternally forsaken being.

Monkey Flower Ode

O, when the space between the necks of purple
grasses, or gazing down at a puzzle of dry brown
leaves; how the sky near my feet brings depth
to the felt sense of things.

O, when the young buck drops an antler by the side
of the path, and the yellow-eyed blackbird pecks at
my head so fiercely she parts my hair!

When the town square turns on its head
and the monkey flower kisses the frown off an
angry woman's face, I am reminded of this time and
place being a crossroads—one world flatly
misunderstood—and the other, from where they
pierce the veil, dropping clues that I am only

one single, buzzing, ecstatic entry in the
indescribable; grateful to have witnessed
the origin of all human knowledge—emerged
from earth's body, to where it returns.

We are all held within the eternal resounding
harmonic.

Larger Than in Life

My father wore black suits with white shirts
and long ties when I used to look up to him.
Water passed over, funneled down the hall,
and washed my father away.

He stood tall in the blue pool in his black suit,
having exceptionally broad shoulders, a bold,
long-boned face and an uncanny, other-worldly
presence (none of which were like him at all).

By dawn, blackbirds were found conversing on
my father's grave. I don't know how, but he
faltered, yet when they lifted his body from the
water, he was a larger man than he'd been in life.

I have to reach so far back for the child, who
saw her father as God or husband, who gave him
count-to-ten-kisses in his blue Lincoln, as it
idled in her mother's driveway.

The cloaked and hooded redwoods, the plum tree
in the yard, and the movie houses he haunted must
have seen him, though no witnesses recall his
statuesque features and fearless gaze, past anything
human, standing tall in the water before he died.

Cul-de-sac

Russet potatoes hang in wire baskets against
patio glass. One drop of persistent rain puddles
outside the door. A lemon tree presses too
close to the window.

One child reads Uncle Remus on a mattress
placed on the living room floor; the other
pulls my robe wanting graham crackers.

On the window ledge, wild persimmons rest
warming in winter sun. The hills are newly
green from soaking up long absent wet.

In the arbor, bluebirds drink from pungent
grapes, loosely threaded to the vine; suburban
maples rage a vibrant red, their uniform placement
like circus tents, ruffles the sidewalk, flamboyant
leaves adorning the street.

In a nearby orchard, the children and I pick walnuts,
passing the park, where migratory
geese etch the pond's surface, imploring.

Along the Pond

Perched one-legged on a stone, the great blue
heron tends the shoreline, then rises, skating over
the pond, slapping the surface with her silver-blue
wings and balking at her long, rippling shadow
as she arcs upward.

On the far shore, Canada geese flee low branches.
The snowy egret tracks silver flashes on the
trembling surface. Mallards dip their iridescent
heads into the glittering.

The cormorant whips the back waters, fanning his
sleek black form past low clouds, pressing his way
into the deep blue belly of the sky.

Camp Solo

An abalone moon floods the meadow, where
a coastal breeze gives sway to a rhythmic,
rocking limb. The foghorn bellows, ushers
memory of early travel by ship across the sea;
scintillating, summer air wafts; waves thrash
against cliffs below. A bright moon casts schools
of opal fish through the trailer window, as into
the open mouth pours the hungry sea. Her cool
cheek turns as she drifts to sleep, exchanging
purpose for dream; and nightbirds, all but one,
settle silently into the sleep of trees.

Old School

In an abandoned classroom, all but the suggestion of light is erased from the chalk-attic air.

The room reeks of spilled wings, artifacts of unquestioned order, crumbling chalk, phantom materials in ink-worn drawers, the lassitude of desks, and a listless assembly of moths fluttering dust-bitten, performing their dance of disappearance.

Was she not supposed to notice the vital ink x'd from the teacher's eyes, his alien gaze past her? Was she there as witness, or was she the insubstantial material that light ignores as it passes through—she who perches idly on her high-legged stool, in judgment of others who failed to answer to the truth of their lives?

From the dull cadence of bodies adrift, the faceless faces dissolving in spidery air, it felt as if no one—not one of us—was truly there.

Early Light

Along the sleepy edge of the pond,
furled spirals of red-orange poppies blaze,
as I cross the shade and am suddenly placed.

When the world that never left opens,
I emerge from the hanging leaves,
startled by the hawk's cry.

In the water, seven turtles float, as if
they had always been there, only now
do I see their fertile display.

Witness

I watched you move to the window, as though
for you, there was no other choice but to rise from
the mother ground like a fish spit out thrashing

from the spiraling current; dropping down to the
place where you see beyond the pane, waiting with
stoic pride before anything is answered.

I saw you standing, poised on the ledge between
two worlds, unable to fall to either side, a tightrope
walker, expert at spirals and catching yourself in

mid-air, when, at the sight of your cheek touching
the window, a mute thing moved in my chest, like a
dormant creature cracking a foot through the egg
wall, voicing its first cry, and

I could make of it only that this felt sense was of the
heart being born—a wordless rapture never before
experienced, and numinous in its
                                awakening.

… III. Portals

Ode to Dream

Dream gives you sudden mechanical genius,
one operational wing, your own way of seeing.

Dream conducts the random, the rhythmic
clacking of invention—hollowed seagrass turned

didgeridoo—jute-strung, hung from the scallop-
backed chair in which you captain your ship

by rubber rudder, claiming agency over your own
mode of nocturnal travel, rising past the

predictable. Had you not dreamed, a barren entry
would have been left in the lineage of the

indescribable, the impossible, and had you not
pressed your feet into the earth—not pressed on—

you would never have known how your beauty
shaped all moments before and after the dream.

Found Object

After lunch at Carmen's, we walked the dogs at
the graveyard. The subject arose as to how we
wanted to be packaged for the hereafter.

I said, *I'd rather be burned than buried, though
I haven't given it much thought. The how of it
changes for me every year,* you said.

We both agreed that bodies need a means of
disposal. Veering off-path to inspect a stone,
I spotted a pristine black and white striped feather,

seemingly placed there for my eyes only,
rested in the dry brown leaves. I said, *From a
pileated Woodpecker, I suspect.*

Strange, they don't typically give up their feathers,
you said. We agreed it was a lucky find: *Auspicious.*

We walked on, amongst the old stones and
their sunken stories, around thick, sculpted granite
blocks shrouded in thousand-year-old lichen,
covering the chiseled text of names.

Release of the Missing Piece

In search of her shoes or the perfect fit,
suddenly she saw that nothing had been
lost or taken from her, so she began to skip,
dreaming herself whole under the moon's
ecstatic gaze.

O cleverly invented illusion!
O, for what the body wants!

She saw that what she had was not less
than what was lost to her, there being no
other to keep from being found but herself.

O, for a life pushing this ragged apple cart!

Released from the stranglehold of False
Promise, the marble edifice slid off its
pedestal of sand. No longer the object of her
hopelessness, he too was set free.

Wooden Stars

She read Zelda, The Female Eunuch, and
Fear of Flying; began a lifetime habit of therapy,
and moved to Santa Cruz to start a new life.

Trading one confused station for another, she
chased men she'd made into stars, yet dodged her
shadow form, persistently flogged by a stern,
shaming light. Yet, however much misguided,
she was an avid stuntman at escaping danger, with
its small cars and imminent callers.

Carrying her net of wooden stars, she scurried bare
legged down narrow halls, sure the men she
dreamed up were chasing her, wanting more than
her car, despite her disheveled hair.

It wasn't until she came to the last door, at the end
of a long dark hall, holding the memory of her
father's sky blue '65 Valiant convertible—her first
car—and easing it down along the oil-spotted floor,
that she realized how small, no bigger than a toy,
her life had been.

In the pause between turns at Simulacrum's
window, as light refracts off a chiseled star, she is
shown in dream her body—a rising flurry of ash—
opiate for the updraft.

Hamilton Cove

Sand and sea scrubbed of all but the toehold—
tendon, muscle, bone, and tooth surrendered
to the sea. The self flushed out.

Below harbor boats, along the sandy shore,
open clam shells, oysters, barnacles, churned-up
crab claws, the pearly interiors of mussel shards,
purple snail shells:

How will death come? No longer imitating life,
at home in exile when the vestibule is pried open,
the staid heel of the body, unfastened,
leaving only an iridescent reverie,

the closing eye of the sun.

Portal of Inevitability

Imagine how it would be to hold one real
Question without fear and despair over
what we do not know.

Human extinction has its advantages.
No needless destruction brought on by
human will. The universe will be free to
reveal itself without riddle or disguise.

Through the portal of inevitability,
one can find their seat at the table, 6 AM,
staring at a placard for Olympia beer,
joined now only by the numberless
who have swallowed their days.

Here on earth, we remain captivated
by violence, and shock headlines, such as
the one about a young city employee,
on trial for tossing his pregnant wife from
a small boat into a man-made lake.
Though, he claims he was just fishing.

Wherever the mind goes after you die,
with human will exhausted, the universe
can then be free to unleash
                      its eternally happy dogs.

For Silence

Hawk gliding along a rib of wind . . .
Touch melting the body's ice . . .
The sad aftermath of media debate . . .
Despair beneath painted surfaces
                        of amateur repair . . .
Water falling, breaking the surface of itself . . .
Time face down without hands . . .
A kiss that satisfies any need for composure . . .
Lifting, as if on cue, into a theatrical sky:

cormorant
            heron
                      hawk
                                crow
                                          dragonfly.

All the World

Chalk rose light, dusk waits for me.
Straw grasses wait. Oak, firmly rooted, waits.
Pond, train full of lumber, evening sparrow—
all wait for me to arrive. Spotted cow,
steeples of flickering aspen, rickety barns
on the mauve-blue hillside—all they want
is what they have. Eucalyptus, angelic choir,
darkening sky, morning bridge, anyone's cry—
all the world asks of me to enter.

Borderland

A room fills with light,
a vast convergence of silence,
intersecting planes, shades
of somersaulting cloud.

A wide window opens onto
resonant blues, seven white sails
below the horizon, a singing sky.

With one foot in dream, what
storms raged are now past.

I lay down in that thrum of brightness
on the heartwood floor, and gazing
skyward through angled glass,
my vision laid bare, fall

headlong into the open-throated sky,
tethered in flight to a red-tailed hawk,
her banner of wings soaring
avenues of softly arced wind.

I Dream of the Last Resort

Light flickers in an upper story window.
Could it be the head cook watching over
the deserted lodge, extending a meal to
a wayfarer, hope to the hopeless?

In a three-sided shack, a yellow cat sleeps
with one eye open, curled in a wood slat box.

I'm passing through. Though, something
tells me this is my piece of earth—my body,
my gray-green bark, my sloping armature,
my tangled overgrowth, my circling, murky
eddy at the passage to the delta,

where I'll swim upstream one day, like the salmon,
join ancestors, as the sun drops out of sight.

How to Argue with Time

Claim it doesn't exist. Toss your clock, your watch-stop, your canary cage. Walk to your internal metronome. Be the why of the turkey crossing the road. Count from infinity backward to the present. Pluck the strands of wild white wires from your good-enough head. Shower the world with what your two hands are capable of. Rock yourself awake. Unleash the rage around your heart. Dance more than not at all. Find eternity in a grain of sand. Name differences. Lick an exotic bird stamp, stick it on a love letter you write to yourself. Begin your ascent as the mountain descends. Open with Upon a Dream and then live it. Make sweet potato pie. Melt the image of Dali's clock. Play Moonlight Sonata on the cello as you did in fifth grade. Be the stones tumbling in the rock polisher till smooth.

Between Rooms

We met between rooms,
between co-abiding and the door.

I stood facing where you'd been
before, to see who you were,

as if memory could bolt us to the floor;
now, vestige of the shore, as you thin to

a hint of catapulting stars—as I too
begin to rise, tethered to a being,

whose great undulating wings—
like bones of light rising will soon

ferry me past the known.

To My Daemon

I catalog the keys of this house—
inscribe a branch with longing.

Foraging through thickets of forgotten
dream, my single beacon fans across
the coal-black night.

Reveling in the bloom of the day lily, I stand
balanced midstream on a chunk of basalt,
my cry shaking the tops of forest trees.

In a world undivided, I study your stillness,
how you sleep, and from where comes
such exquisite singing. When we met again,

immersed in the dark-jeweled loam,
we will greet each other as familiars—
not by name or word, but by

warm hand in warm hand,
                singing each other home.

The Potter

In the potter's field, only hunger and exhaustion
remain at the end of a long day.

To the man that lives in the house that looks out
upon the field of summer barley, the sight means
almost as much as it did when he was a young boy,
there would be enough grain for the winter to come.

It pains the man to crush the rock he hauls from the
woods and river; surrendering stone after stone to
the mechanical jaw, destroying their manifold maps,
their storied mineral striations, and grinding all to
powder, for the clay that will turn his potter's wheel.

For his granduncle in his time, the same wild
grasses were the long, yellow strands of a woman's
hair.

Now, the man is a grandfather, still content with his
garden's bounty; able to work the earth,
so closely at times as to feel indistinguishable from
the bucket of straw-colored feldspar, the hammer
leaned against the wall next to it.

Yet, when that early room in memory shades to a
darkening gray, from that incomprehensible sense
of loss, silence strikes so hard it fractures the air
into shards . . .

For that boy of five, and for the father he became,
he recollects once more, how his own father went
forever missing in the war.

Crossroads

One night in my twenties, driving in a blackout,
I came to, in the middle of a dirt road. Just over the
top of a presenting hill, headlights glared, then the
car barreled down the centerline. I must
have swerved out of the way just in time.

These days, I pedal a Townie electric; a remake of
the old commuter bike with its voluminous air-filled
tires, wire basket, curved handlebars,
a "spirit bell," and a wide seat for my wide ass.

If I ever again get lost after the sun goes down,
I have one gleaming bulb that crowns my
front wheel—its bright moonish beam ever-
prepared to fan back the ubiquitous edge of night.

Though some days echo that old dark despair;
this feathery light I ride into, I choose to call a
guiding one—flickering at the crossroads,
yet obstinately my own.

The Myth of Me

I no longer run from men who want me dead,
or leap through windows, shattering glass.

No tidal waves wash over me, no more veering off
radical cliffs in out-of-control cars.

Now, when I cross a man who's drunk or bluffing,
I grab his buck knife. Now, I make heroic dives

into green pools of crime, swim through cattails
past sleeping bullfrogs. Undistracted by the

unbroken monologue of the phantom lifeguard,
I rise from the slippery algae.

I may be only a cartoon hero who's called to
dematerialize evil, zapping the villain with the

black-hook mustache, by insight alone. And you
might find me in the darkest sky, hovering above

an urban alleyway, noting a tenant's disgruntled
worship of their faltering plumbing.

I imagine there will always be situations, like this,
worthy of my intervention.

Wire Bird

for Jonqui

Streaming downriver, you keep rowing.
Tethered to your wire birds, you are going.
A city girl, crossing sidewalk cracks.
Kinder now, you still shun the grass.
Flame hair redyed for its final showing.

Fallen camelia, to where are you flowing?
Everywhere or just nowhere for posing?
Post fall, cut flowers arrived like claps.
Streaming downriver, you keep rowing.

Your sister stays by you, daughter coping.
Flickering silence, innocence dozing.
Droplets of time we know can't last.
Coming closer to breath's final pass.
Soon you'll be gone with no foreboding.
                Down rivers of sky, black butterfly.

Truth Is Darkest

when you don't change the script.
What would I be without a body?

I said, you are part of my lineage.
You laughed—we touched hands.

What would I be without a body?
I drove my car into the water,

You laughed—we touched hands.
I am an animal with no name.

What would I be without a body?
There is a door beneath everything, you said.

I drove my car into the water.
I'd been a walking shadow of all I saw.

You laughed—we touched hands.
I said, you are part of my lineage.

I am an animal with no name.
Truth is darkest when

you don't change the script.

You Are Not Lost

You are here. Slide your hands under her head; make of them a cradle. Stop repeating the myth about love and success that will land in your lap or evade you forever . . . feel the draw of breath. Anchor your seat and feet. Follow where the head wants to roll. From midline, rock on the sitzbones. There is nothing more glorious on the face of the earth than someone who refuses to give up. Build a humble, flawed life. Track the breath as your fingertips find the soft notch of the occiput. Nothing is more fabulous than someone who refuses to give in to their most self-hating, discouraged, disillusioned self. Let the weight of her head fall back onto the pads of your fingertips. Relish the feeling of building a hut in the middle of the suffocating dust. Cherish this.

Around the Corner

You are slowly moving into the great neighborhood
of the beyond. Little did you know that it was right
around the corner from where you've been living all
this time, but today, your wheels—like wings—took
you there, while you were on your way to elsewhere.
You love this old place, somehow familiar, as if you'd
always yearned to live here—how had you missed it?
Today, the rain kisses the simple houses, the lichen-
breasted fence, the moss-covered brick path, the scatter
of brown leaves. Today, you gently press your palm
to your breast and vow to begin, again and
again, no matter what.

Aperture

Dark empties you, fills you with its deep sympathy, spreads a starlit blanket of simplicity overall. Yet when you wake, you forget its equalizing wellspring tapped in the night. You wake as if never emptied, never carried, never fully embraced, and you begin immediately to soil the cloth. Those early emissaries of dawn warn you to keep an eye on the coming light. Yet you relinquish all that weightlessness, begin to ruminate, compare, calculate—the old self-betrayal . . . without a breath between, you close the aperture on promise, on mystery, on equanimity. If you could only catch yourself again and again as you turn your back.

Paean

The rose has nothing on the peony, though
they may share the same vase, in which

from their common fate, the peony exhales
sublime efflorescence in her final bloom.

She casts her confetti to the wind, though cut—
even with a calloused stem—the severed foot.

A healer comes by horseback with her satchel
of charms: herbs, salve, gems…for prophecy,

I propose—to soften the stone hearts of women
like me, who sew poems into our clothes.

Like women, whose poems stitch and expose,
how the rose has nothing on the peony.

Make My Day

Remember The Good, Bad, and the Ugly?

When Clint Eastwood was a young cowboy and when going to a matinee was exciting, coming in out of the blue, into the musky dark theater with mostly empty seats?

The exercise is to write about my muse. Why did I start here? My muse hangs out in some liminal sphere between excitement and surprise and especially on Tuesdays when

I have nothing special planned and decide to do something I haven't done since I was a teenager—like having a picnic on a small lake and bringing the I Ching.

My muse doesn't appear like anyone, though she could be any possibility. Perhaps she's a friend that joins me, someone I haven't yet met. I make room for her presence.

Perhaps she is partly a memory of innocence in a sea of guilty charges and chaotic ramblings, I invite her to stay as I haven't written anything new since last year and since today is Tuesday, a day to walk outside and smell the grass or finger a tree's bark still wet from excessive rain.

Often, she's a cat who draws me in as one of her kin. She wants to share her treasures with me, those visible and invisible—rock, wood, boxes, berry, patches of ground warm with sun.

Curious as wind, she craves the spaces between the petals of a rose, between twigs and a snake's shed skin, between clouds and the wheat field, between hands and honeypots.

What do you name this formless jester who is also sometimes form and who is constantly moving through you though you are often stuck in your skull. Let her tell you her name. Maybe Squink, maybe Squill.

Up the Inside Passage

On a ferry up the Inside Passage, I knit-purled
a coral-colored sweater. Only this time, I was
the doll, turned inside out and unraveling.

Alert for clues of salvation, I sailed north,
carrying keys with a jingle of little note.
Only I was the doll, turned inside and unraveling.

Even so, I was amazed to find myself nowhere.
I had to get my money back to anchor these buckling bones.

Ashamed by my lack of self-dominion, yet
A premonition told me to run as fast as I could

from the thief, whose secret revealed itself
only after I'd signed the paperwork, when he
extended his hook-for-hand for me to shake.

Carrying keys with a jingle of little note,
I had to get my money back. Alert for clues of

salvation, I sailed north. But the merit came
too late. On a ferry up the Inside Passage,

I knit-pearled a coral-colored sweater.
Determined to get my money back for
anchoring these buckling bones.

Welcome This Artifact

Welcome to this artifact, one record of the movement of mind.
Welcome the common dishevelment of one human day,
light as a tremulous glint of wavering flickers.

Welcome the common dishevelment of one human day.
This fabled existence, these myths of awakening.
Welcome the moon as the dark and light of creation.

Welcome this fabled existence, the beckoning avian call.
Rock the moon as the dark and light of creation.
Welcome the cat's yowl of longing in the predawn.

Welcome light as a tremulous glint of wavering flickers.
The cat's yowl of longing in the predawn.
Welcome this artifact, one record of the movement of mind.

Another COVID Day

Spread out on a café table, the obituaries . . .

A pastor was struck down while riding his bike. I can see him rolling out of the garage into the ivy green shade to the cool newly repaved road, a morning light splicing through the redwoods. He thought he was prepared, with his Apple watch with the app for tracking wheel revolutions, wearing his skintight sky-blue shorts, the number 78 in bold on the back of his matching shirt.

Beverly died of cancer. The announcement reveals the day of her death but excludes her birth. So, an old woman dies yet her identifying picture is one from her high school graduation, in pearls, her face smooth as glass. What a shame it would be to present the newly dead precisely the age they were in all their testimony and triumph, traces of interpersonal weariness and (say it) decrepitude.

A woman I went to graduate school with, a poet and singer songwriter, died suddenly, emphasis on suddenly.

My sister-in-law's mother died of COVID at its onset, in a nursing home; her daughter forbidden to be with her.

I had to put my dog down; she was inconsolable.
I couldn't tell if it was pain. She'd been pacing for two years, yet even towards the end, in a calm moment, she would approach me as I sat on the couch reading and lick the flesh of my knee.

Where are all the dead? The mass graves?
The public memorials?

Enshrined

On a paltry shelf, jars blaze obtuse.
Quan Yin reclines on her tarnished metal shrine.
Day after day, I become of less use.

Why run a household? Such self-abuse.
Dishes lay in the sink growing vines.
On a paltry shelf jarred goods blaze obtuse.

After years without wine, I find an excuse.
Still hoping to reap from a glitter-mine.
Day after day, I become of less use.

Even the keys go in search of a lock to let loose.
The box goes in search of a lid.
On a paltry shelf jarred goods blaze obtuse.

The window yawns, yearns for new views.
The door wants only to open, by design.
Day upon day, I become old news.

Kids long grown. Gone. Vows, a ruse.
My life flattens, stuck to destiny's shrine.
Jarred goods blaze obtuse
and day after day, I become of less use.

Bardo

You are brave enough to live your dying.
Everyone sends flowers as if you're already gone.
Choiceless, there is only waiting.
Like a swan whose neck is listening.
Or a stark silence gazing at grass blades.

I recall my first yellow cat.
Now, wishing time wouldn't run out.
What light are you bleeding toward?

In the grammar of omission, the bad man flies off.
Nobody gets free without breaking.
My long gestating heart still fidgets.
This swan's neck is a fountain's cast stone.

Called to task for all I should know.
Beyond just getting old and my gold-yellow cat.
What name did your flame red hair never reveal?
Unravelling the pattern's secret sensibility,

Eyes with whole bodies inside them.
Unsung birds are an invitation, a mixed revelation.
What must die for me to live?
Asks the stone wrapped in ode.

My cat licks the rain from her paw.
Call me old enough to know.
Learning comes in spirals, like it doesn't show.
Silence before dawn, then the drumming of water.

I am an animal with no name.
Song is the *shadow hearing* of sound.
Death is in the room. The river shrinks under duress.
Unravelling, the pattern is a mixed revelation.

The moon, a stone wrapped in cloud.
Pink carnival tissue floats in a petri dish of lost connection.

Reverse Gravity

When the moon's opal gaze broadcasts over
the ginkgo tree's fan-shaped leaves, loosening
the bonds of physicality—gravity reverses.

With concise effort and precise levity, she lifts
into the sky. Sense-radiant—an ear the current
streams through, a whorled imprint fingering
the cleft of river rock,

the hawk's eye spanning the horizon.

About the Author

Centa Therese has work in many journals, including *Tower* (audio collages), *Meridian, Pisgah Review, Harpur Palate, Hurricane Review, Eclipse,* and *DrumVoices Revue*. Her poem "Night Gardening" is forthcoming in *Ploughshares* in 2026.

She has authored the letterset edition *Blameless Recognition of Natural Light* (Clamshell Press, 2022) and the lyric memoir *The Illuminated Field; Cultivating a Small World* (independently published, 2014). Additionally, she edited *Becoming Athena: Poems by Women in Recovery* (independently published, 2024).

Centa is a language arts educator, a photoartist, a Neuroaffective Touch practitioner, and a Creative Resilience coach. Her collection of prose poems, *Night Gardening,* is currently a semi-finalist with Sixteen Rivers Press.

Visit her websites:
centatherese.com
centatheresestudios.com

www.ingramcontent.com/pod-product-compliance
Lightning Source LLC
Chambersburg PA
CBHW030910170426
43193CB00009BA/804